Neskorodev S.N. The ankle trips and trips in wing chun

Wing Chun is a system of active defense and attack, characterized by short explosive attacks by hands, low kicks by legs and synchronous attack and defense. Like most martial systems, Wing Chun doesn't limit itself in using blows by hands (by fist, elbows, palm and palm rib), legs, head or knees. Beside the striking technique, Wing Chun uses the throwing and pain technique (cin-na). The ankle trips and other forms of adversary's balance disturbance are also the part of Wing Chun art. The section of ankle trips in Wing Chun is not elucidated in detail, because it is related to the masterful level.

At that the ankle trips and trips are the severe arm in the arsenal of Wing Chun master. Wing Chun master uses any mistakes in stand, in weight distribution, in displacements by using ankle trips. The adversary loses balance and falls in most unexpected moments, most often at own attacks. Even if the ankle trip doesn't result in adversary's fall, the masters use them as an element of more complex attack. In such case the ankle trip plays an auxiliary role – transfers the adversary's attention down, at legs level, and the master's attack is realized at the upper one, left without the adversary's attention. This book is devoted to the ankle trips and trips in Wing Chun.

Copyright © 2017 Neskorodev S.
Author: S. Neskorodev

ISBN-13: 978-1544954226

ISBN-10: 1544954220

All rights reserved. No part of this book may be reproduced or transmitted in any form or by any means, electronic or mechanical, including photocopying, recording, or by any information storage and retrieval system, without permission in writing from the copyright owner.

THE BIOMECHANICAL GROUNDS OF HOLDS BY LEGS 3

The fighter's biomechanical model 3
The destruction of balance at ankle trips and trips 7
The main ways of disturbance of balance by hands 9
The biomechanics of ankle trips 18
The biomechanics of trips 22
The biomechanics of grabs 25
The biomechanics of hooks 28
The ankle trips and bridges building 31
The ankle trips and "sticky hands" technique 33
The use of adversary's force at ankle trips 35

THE SIDE ANKLE TRIP 41

THE ANKLE TRIP FROM INSIDE 51

THE FRONT ANKLE TRIP 62

THE BACK ANKLE TRIP BY KICK 64

THE BACK TRIP 68

THE FRONT TRIP 80

THE GRAB 85

THE EXTERNAL HOOK 91

THE INTERNAL HOOK 101

THE BIOMECHANICAL GROUNDS OF HOLDS BY LEGS

The fighter's biomechanical model

Before considering the holds, used by Wing Chun masters, it is necessary to pay attention to the main notions of biomechanics. It is important to understand the essence of ankle trips and trips in Wing Chun. The human organism is in certain perspective the mechanical system that is consists of certain elements – bones, joints, tendons, muscles that all together provide the movement of this system. For describing the biomechanical model of ankle trips and trips in Wing Chun, it is necessary to define the main notions, related to the technique of holds. There are:

1. The body gravity center.
2. The support of biomechanical.
3. The foothold area (steadiness zone)
4. The body structure.

The body gravity center (body center) is a conventional point, placed in the belly center, which position characterizes the balance of the whole body. At making ankle trips and trips the fighter must consciously manage the adversary's body center and elaborate such technique of blows, blocks, grips, that affects the adversary's body center.

The support of biomechanical system is determined by the stand force and legs force. Legs hold the body weight. The fighter's (biomechanical system) steadiness depends on how firmly they are standing on earth. In martial arts as a whole and in Wing Chun in particular the attention is accented on the fact that the fighter must confidently stand on earth, must have the firm support. In Eastern styles such body (mechanical system) ability is often named rooting or earthing. At making ankle trips it is necessary to deprive the adversary of support on earth. If the fighter loses the one of supports, he loses balance at non-distributed gravity center.

The foothold area (steadiness zone) is a conventional zone, the area between fighter's legs. If the body center projection falls on this zone, the biomechanical system is stable. If the body center projection goes beyond the foothold area, the system loses balance.

The foothold area can be conventionally divided in eight directions – forward, back, to the right, to the left, diagonally forward, diagonally back, diagonally to the right and diagonally to the left. It is important for understanding the mechanisms of taking adversary out of balance and making ankle trips.

The body center projection is a conventional perpendicular, lowered from the body center on earth. At the stable rooted stand the fighter's body center projection falls on the foothold area center. The fighter's position is stable, if perpendicular, lowered from his body gravity center, doesn't go beyond the foothold area. On the figure is presented the high side stand, the body weight is distributed evenly on both legs, the body mass center projection falls on the middle of foothold area that provides steadiness.

If the body center projection on foothold area is displaced, the fighter loses balance. The closer is the body center projection to the outer boundary of foothold area, the less steady the fighter is. Such situations can appear in the combat dynamics. The general rule for keeping balance is the following thesis: *the body center projection must not go beyond the foothold area (steadiness zone). If the body center projection goes beyond the foothold area (steadiness zone), the fighter*

loses balance that can result in fall. So, the general rule for making ankle trips and trips is taking the adversary's body center projection out of foothold area (steadiness zone).

The examples of taking the adversary's body center projection out of foothold area are presented below and described further in the book.

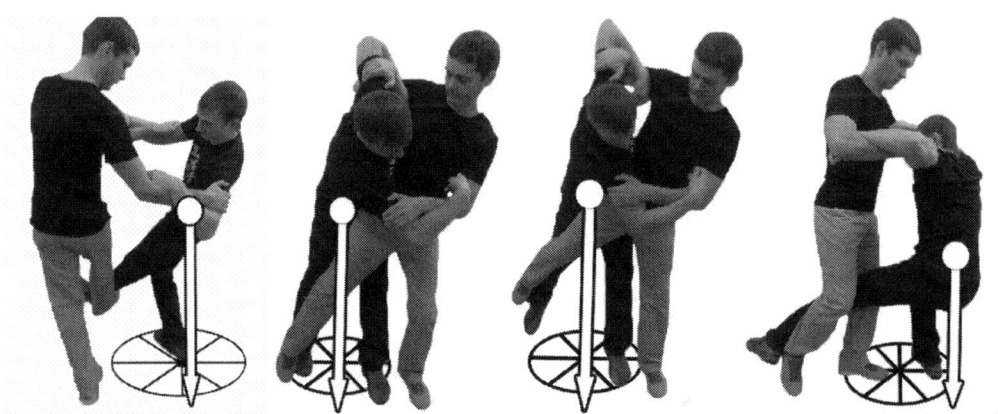

The internal body structure is a totality of bones, joints, tendons and muscles of the body that provide the internal integrity of fighter's body. At disturbance of the structure integrity the steadiness of stand is lost. The structure can be disturbed by blows, kicks, holds, jerks, pushes. The affect on adversary's structure affects also his body center that creates preconditions for making ankle trips and trips.

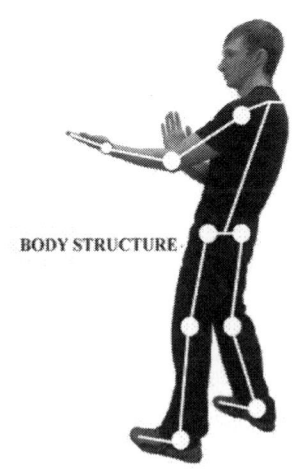

The destruction of balance at ankle trips and trips

Each Wing Chun fighter must study the main ways of balance destruction, used for making ankle trips and trips. The fighters must pay attention to the study of preparation for throws no less than to the study of throws. The mastership of Wing Chun fighter is expressed in ability to create the favorable conditions for making throw. His actions must force the adversary to lose balance for any moment, to stand on one leg or to deviate in any side in such a way that his body gravity center goes beyond the foothold area. Intensifying this movement of adversary, the fighter must make throw in direction of his deviation or, using the resistance, offered by the adversary for restoring balance, to make throw in opposite direction.

For training the skill of disturbance of balance in Wing Chun there is a preparatory training exercise. Its execution allows training persons to acquire skills of disturbance of balance and to study the main directions of taking out of balance.

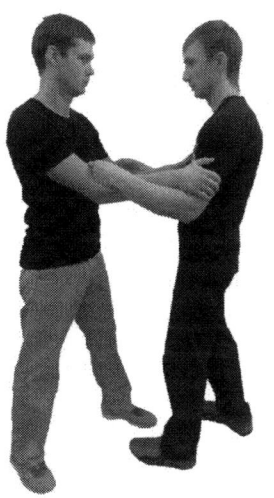

For executing this exercise the practicing persons stand in front of each other in side stands. They extend hands forward and put hands on elbow bends of each other. The partner, who'll train the disturbance of balance (first number), puts hands on elbow bends of other partner from inside. It is more comfortable for grip and control of partner's structure that is why such grip is made by the first partner, who trains the disturbance of balance. So, the hands of second partner are outside. The initial position for this exercise is shown on the figure.

Before describing this exercise, let's consider the schematic figure that helps to understand the biomechanical sense of taking the adversary's structure out of balance. The top view of the partner's stand is schematically presented on the figure below. The circle is the foothold area. The point in the center is the body center projection on foothold area. The lines within circle mean eight main directions of disturbance of adversary's structure balance.

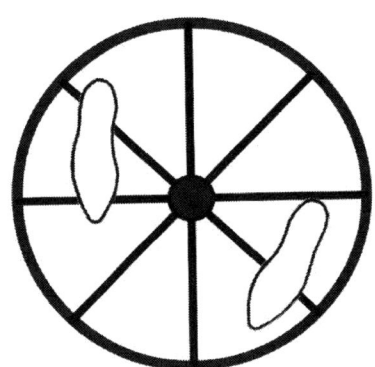

Depending on how the fighter affects the partner's structure, his body center projection on foothold area will displace in one of eight possible directions. Let's consider all eight possible ways of disturbance of balance that will be used in further for making ankle trips and trips. On the figures below we can see the change of body (gravity) center projection on foothold area at disturbance of balance. The black point within the circle marks the displacement of body center and the loss of partner's balance.

The main ways of disturbance of balance by hands

The disturbance of balance directly forward

The practicing persons stand in front of each other in side stands and elbow grips. The fighter realizes the throw of partner's structure on himself. The partner's body center rises up and moves directly forward. The body weight is transferred on toes, the heels are separated from the floor. The partner loses connection with earth and rooting, the force of stand becomes weak. On schematic figure is shown how the partner's body center projection (black point) moves directly forward within the foothold area (big circle) that reflects the loss of partner's balance. After jerk and taking out of balance the fighter returns partner in initial position. It must be repeated the necessary number of times for mastering.

The disturbance of balance directly back

The practicing persons stand in front of each other in side stands and elbow grips. The fighter makes push of the partner's structure from himself directly back. The partner's body center moves back. The body weight is transferred on heels, toes are separated from the floor. The partner loses connection with earth and rooting, the force of stand becomes weak. On schematic figure is shown how the partner's body center projection (black point) moves directly back within the foothold area (big circle) that reflects the loss of partner's balance. After jerk and taking out of balance the fighter returns partner in initial position. It must be repeated the necessary number of times for mastering.

The disturbance of balance to the right

The practicing persons stand in front of each other in side stands and elbow grips. The fighter makes jerk of partner's left hand down by the right hand. Synchronously with it the fighter's left hand abruptly rises up, affecting the partner's right forearm. As a result of the work of both fighter's hands the jerk of partner's structure to the right down is realized. The partner's body center is displaced on the left leg, the right leg is released from weight. The body weight is transferred on the left leg, the right one is separated from foothold. The partner loses connection with earth and rooting, the force of stand grows weak. On schematic figure is shown how the partner's body center projection (black point) moves to the right (relative to the fighter) within the foothold area (big circle) that reflects the loss of partner's balance. After jerk and taking out of balance the fighter returns partner in initial position. It must be repeated the necessary number of times for mastering.

The disturbance of balance to the left

The practicing persons stand in front of each other in side stands and elbow grips. The fighter makes jerk of partner's right hand down by the left hand. Synchronously with it the right hand abruptly rises up, affecting the partner's structure through his left forearm. As a result of the work of fighter's both hands the jerk of partner's structure to the left down is realized. The partner's body center is displaced on the right leg, the left leg is released from weight. The body weight is transferred on the right leg, the left one is separated from foothold. The partner loses connection with earth and rooting, the force of stand grows weak. On schematic figure is shown how the partner's body center projection (black point) moves to the left (relative to the fighter) within the foothold area (big circle) that reflects the loss of partner's balance. After jerk and taking out of balance the fighter returns partner in initial position. It must be repeated the necessary number of times for mastering.

The disturbance of balance forward diagonally to the right

The practicing persons stand in front of each other in side stands and elbow grips. The fighter makes jerk of partner's structure on himself and to the right – to the right shoulder. The partner's body center rises up and moves forward and to the right. The body weight is transferred on toes, the heels are separated from the floor. The partner loses connection with earth and rooting, the force of stand grows weak. On schematic figure is shown how the partner's body center projection (black point) moves forward and to the right within the foothold area (big circle) that reflects the loss of partner's balance. After jerk and taking out of balance the fighter returns partner in initial position. It must be repeated the necessary number of times for mastering.

The disturbance of balance forward diagonally to the left

The practicing persons stand in front of each other in side stands and elbow grips. The fighter makes jerk of partner's structure on himself and to the left – to the left shoulder. The partner's body center rises up and moves forward and to the left. The body weight is transferred on toes, the heels are separated from the floor. The partner loses connection with earth and rooting, the force of stand grows weak. On schematic figure is shown how the partner's body center projection (black point) moves forward and to the left within the foothold area (big circle) that reflects the loss of partner's balance. After jerk and taking out of balance the fighter returns partner in initial position. It must be repeated the necessary number of times for mastering.

F

The disturbance of balance back diagonally to the right

The practicing persons stand in front of each other in side stands and elbow grips. The fighter makes push of partner's structure from himself and to the right. The partner's body center moves back and to the right. The body weight is transferred on heels, the toes are separated from the floor. The partner loses connection with earth and rooting, the force of stand grows weak. On schematic figure is shown how the partner's body center projection (black point) moves back and to the right within the foothold area (big circle) that reflects the loss of partner's balance. After push and taking out of balance the fighter returns partner in initial position. It must be repeated the necessary number of times for mastering.

The disturbance of balance back diagonally to the left

The practicing persons stand in front of each other in side stands and elbow grips. The fighter makes push of partner's structure from himself and to the left. The partner's body center moves back and to the left. The body weight is transferred on heels, the toes are separated from the floor. The partner loses connection with earth and rooting, the force of stand grows weak. On schematic figure is shown how the partner's body center projection (black point) moves back and to the left within the foothold area (big circle) that reflects the loss of partner's balance. After push and taking out of balance the fighter returns partner in initial position. It must be repeated the necessary number of times for mastering.

The types of holds by legs

All hold by legs can be divided in four types by their effect on adversary's structure.
1. Ankle trips
2. Trips
3. Grabs
4. Hooks

Each of these holds has common and individual features. The common features include the hands work. The differences concern the methods of affect by legs on adversary's ones. But these differences and classification on practice are often conventional that is many holds can be made in different variations and the boundaries between them are eliminated.

But if made the theoretical differences, the biomechanics of all holds by legs on adversary's ones can be divided in three stages.

On the first stage hands make preparatory effect on adversary's structure, forcing to transfer the body weight on one or another leg. At that the fighter can make auxiliary steps, sub-steps, jumps for changing stand and creating the necessary conditions for holds.

At the second stage the effect of fighter's leg on adversary's one is realized. And the individual features of holds are manifested there.

If the effect is realized on adversary's empty leg (the leg without adversary's weight) by the swing of fighter's leg, it is an ankle trip.

If the affect is realized on adversary's loaded leg (the leg that partially bears the adversary's body weight), by the fighter's leg, set against the foothold (earth), it is a trip.

If the effect is realized on half-loaded or loaded adversary's leg (the leg that bears the adversary's weight) by the swing of fighter's leg, it is a grab.

If the effect is realized on half-loaded or loaded adversary's leg (the leg that bears the adversary's weight) by the back side of fighter's ankle behind the adversary's leg (adversary's leg is hooked), it is a hook.

At the third stage the reworking of hold by hands and trunk take place.

It is a conventional division in stages. In real conditions each hold is realized in one movement and the stages are combined without distinct separation. Thus, the work by hands for the effect on adversary's structure is realized at each of three stages.

At the same time the distinct boundary can't be always put between the holds, especially, between the trips and grabs. The holds often have intermediate variant.

For deciphering each type of holds, let's consider the biomechanics of each of them.

The biomechanics of ankle trips

The adversary is relatively stable in stands. But if apply force (or better two forces) to its structure through the one or two grips, it can result in unsteadiness of adversary's structure in one of eight directions. That is why the actions by hands play very important role in preparation and realization of ankle trips. Obviously, the significance of actions by legs and the whole body must not be underestimated in preparation and realization of throw, but the efforts of attacking person are transferred on adversary only by hands.

Two fighter's hands in grip synchronously apply two force vectors in such a way to take the adversary out of balance. The disturbance of balance is a necessary condition to realize ankle trip. After realization of effect on adversary's structure and taking him out of balance the adversary's body weight is displaced on the one of legs. One leg becomes loaded (full) – the body weight is transferred on it as a result of effect on structure. The second leg becomes empty – it doesn't bear the body weight or is partially released from the body weight. At that the adversary's body center is displaced on the loaded leg. It is a first (preparatory) effect of making ankle trip.

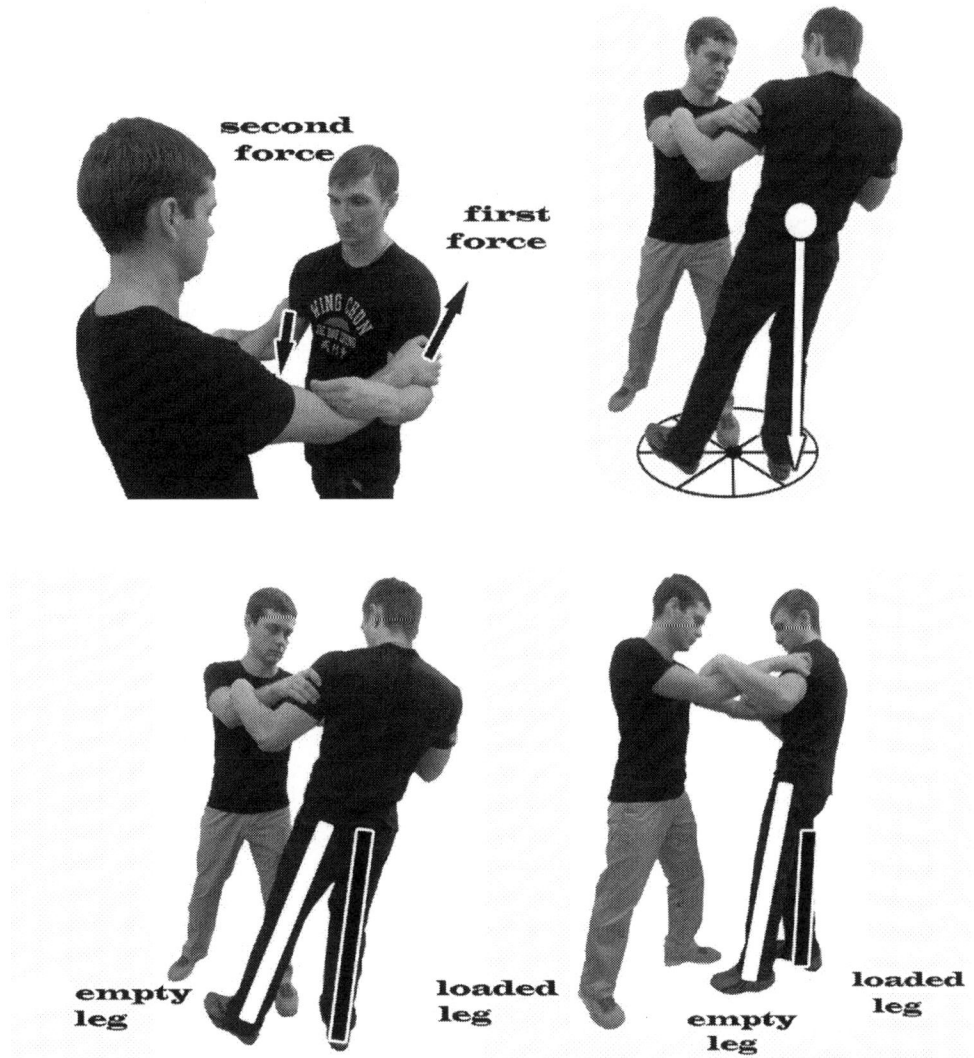

Hands are the connecting link between fighters. The fighter takes the adversary out of balance by short, abrupt movements of hands, gradually adding the efforts of legs and trunk. The fighter must feel the slightest adversary's movements (pull or pressure) and instantly react to them, this quality is trained in exercises "sticky hands", very important in Wing Chun.

At the second (main) stage the affect (undercutting) of adversary's empty leg takes place. The fighter undercuts the adversary's empty leg by his own leg, in such a way eliminating the one of supports. Having been left without the one support, the adversary's body loses balance with fall. If hands are the main connective link with adversary, legs also realize very important function in the combat. They serve as a main mean, stopper, lever that the adversary is crossed through at making trips or that beats the foothold out from under adversary at making ankle trips. For strengthening the undercutting effect by leg, the different steps that give force and allow use the body inertia for undercutting movement can be applied.

The third stage (auxiliary-ending) is the additional work by trunk and hands at undercutting moment. At taking adversary out of balance Wing Chun fighter's trunk plays no lesser role than hands and legs. The upper shoulder girdle at turns and bends acts as a lever, increasing the force and amplitude of hands movements, displaces the body weight beyond the foothold area and affects the adversary by its own weight.

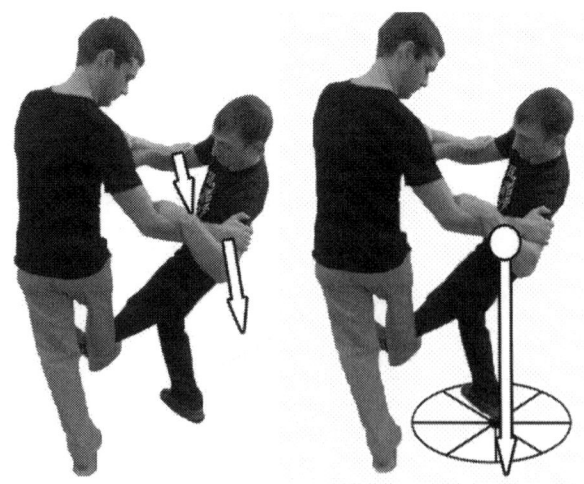

To strengthen the ankle trip and raise its effectiveness the fighter, after undercutting the adversary's empty leg, starts to affect the adversary's structure by hands and upper shoulder girdle in such a way that his body weight is displaced on the empty undercut leg. The adversary's body weight is transferred on the undercut leg, and as far as this leg can't be a support after ankle trip, the adversary falls.

Thus, the general algorithm of any ankle trip can be described in three steps:

1. Preparatory stage – the effect by hands on adversary's structure disturbance of balance, loading of one leg with the weight, release of another one from the weight.

2. Main stage – ankle trip of adversary's empty leg (the leg without weight) by the leg.

3. Final stage – additional effect on adversary's structure by hands, transfer of adversary's body weight on undercut leg.

All three stages are realized together and continuously. Depending on situation, the first and second or the second and third stages can be realized synchronously. The aforesaid scheme is the most general one, giving the general understanding of biomechanics of each type of ankle trip. Depending on the ankle trip type, the biomechanics of hold will be concretized.

During the training and mastering of ankle trips each stage may be executed successively for more detail understanding. At mastering and understanding of holds the speed and unity of stages increase.

At basic (training) perfecting of ankle trips the partner doesn't resist, doesn't manifest any force, but he is as if the living "trainer", "dummy" for training. It is necessary for practicing person to understand the sense and biomechanics of ankle trip. At mastering, the partner can increase resistance.

The biomechanics of trips

Thus, the trip is a hold, at which the effect on adversary's loaded leg is realized by the fighter's one, leant on earth. The trip also needs preparatory work by hands for the effect on adversary's structure. But their aim is quite other. If at ankle trips the main aim is to release one leg from the body weight and transfer it on the other one, the aim of the work by hands at trips, on the contrary, to transfer the adversary's body weight on the leg that the hold will be executed on. In other words, to load the adversary's one or two legs. For example, the fighter can load two adversary's hand by hands movement down or he can load the one adversary's leg by the movement of one hand to the left and other one down (see the figure below). It is the first (preparatory) stage of trip execution.

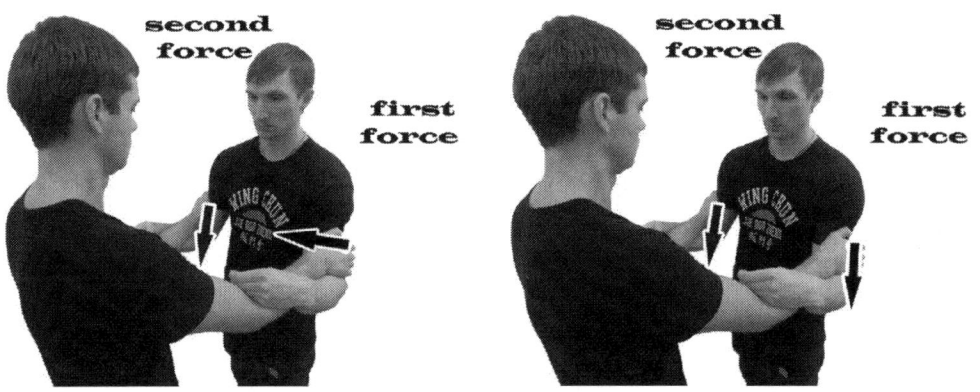

Then the fighter makes preparatory movement by legs for realizing the main effect by leg on adversary's legs. It is the second stage of trip. The right leg makes step forward between the adversary's legs. The left one makes step behind the fighter's right leg and stands from external side of adversary's left leg.

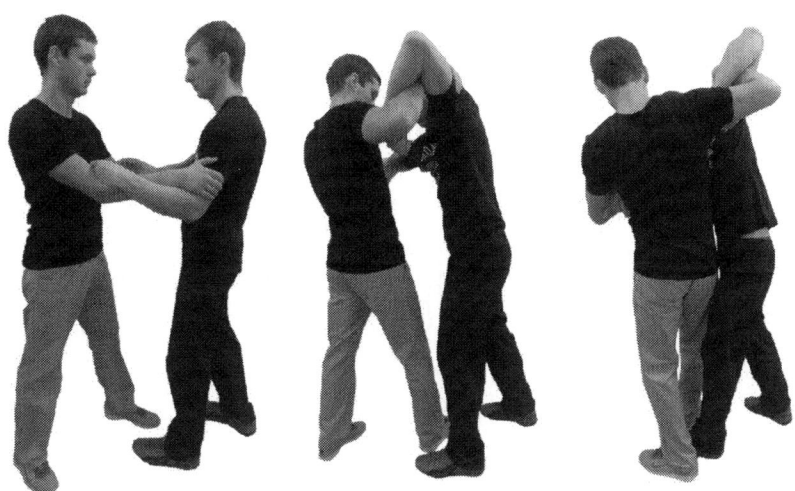

In the final phase of this stage two adversary's legs remain loaded. The fighter puts his right leg as close as possible to the adversary's one and affect it by the abrupt straightening of knee bend (the third force) (see the figure below). At that hands continue to affect the adversary's structure and to pull forward and down. The right leg, put forward, plays the role of obstacle that the adversary stumbles against.

The third stage it is again the additional work by trunk and hands. As a result of three forces action, the adversary's body center goes beyond the foothold area, and adversary loses balance with fall.

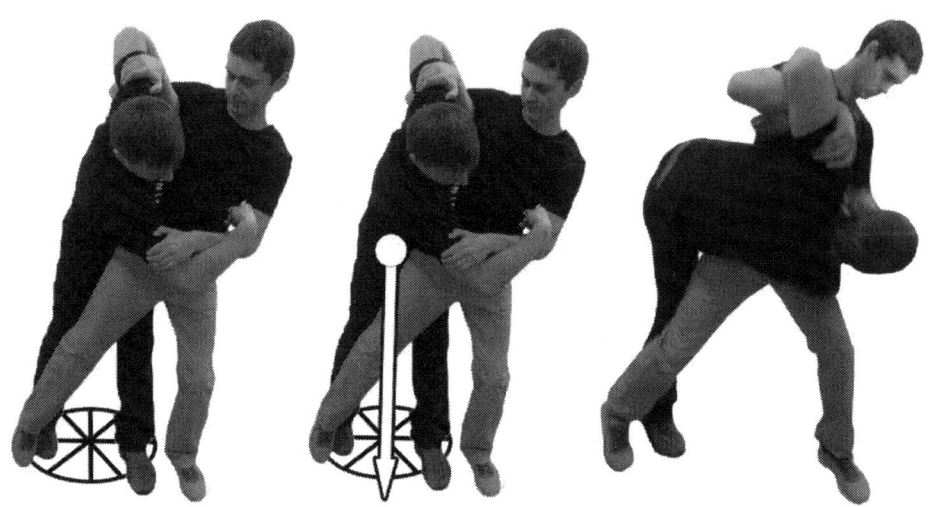

For strengthening the trip and raising its effectiveness the fighter, after the beat of adversary's loaded leg by knee bend, begins to affect the adversary's structure by hands and upper shoulder girdle in such a way that his body weight is displaced beyond the foothold area.

Thus, the general algorithm of any trip may be described in three steps.

1. Preparatory stage – the affect on adversary's structure by hands, disturbance of balance, loading of one or two legs with the weight.

2. Main stage – the setting of trip under adversary's loaded leg (the leg with adversary's body weight), the support on earth by leg, the beat of adversary's loaded leg by knee bend.

3. Final stage – the additional affect on adversary's structure by hands, the transfer of adversary's weight through the fighter's leg that makes trip.

All three stages are realized together and continuously.

The biomechanics of grabs

Thus, the grab is a hold, at which the effect on adversary's half-loaded or loaded leg is realized by the fighter's leg that makes swing. Grabs also need the preparatory work by hands for affect the adversary's structure. The aim of the work by hands at grabs is analogous to the one at trips – to load the adversary's one or two legs. For example, the fighter can load two adversary's leg by hands movement down or he can load the one adversary's leg by the movement of one hand to the left and other one down (see the figure below). It is the first (preparatory) stage of grab execution.

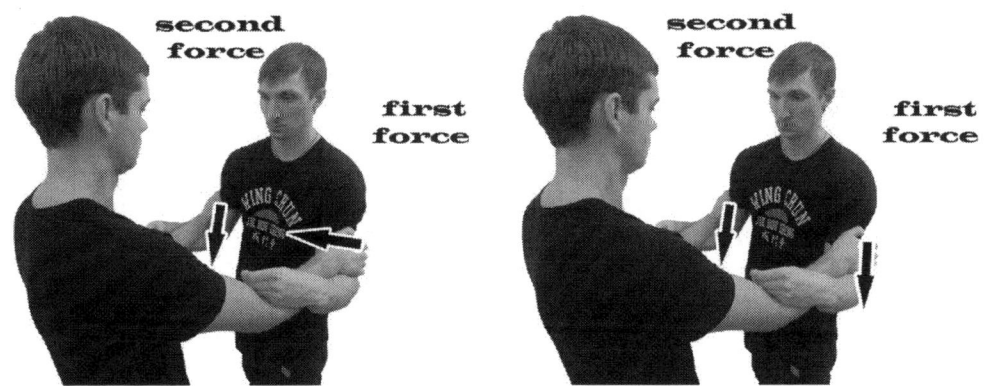

At the second stage of the hold the fighter makes preparatory movement by legs to realize the main effect on adversary's legs by the leg, namely the swing by leg.

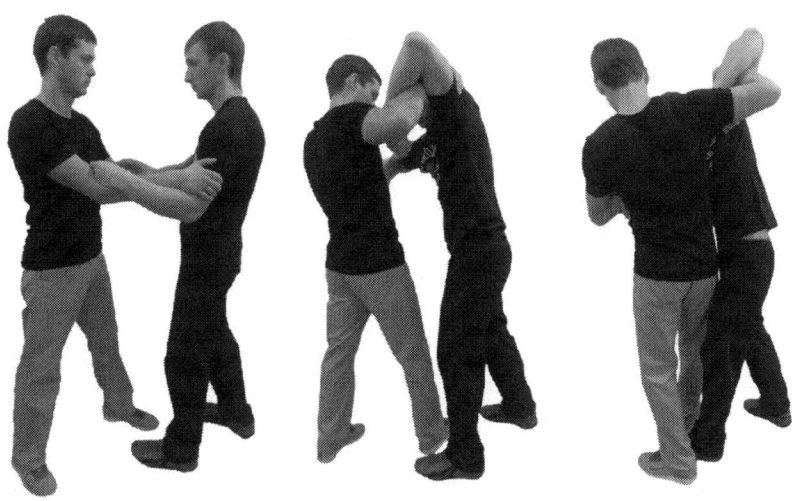

In final stage the adversary's one or two legs remain loaded or half-loaded. The fighter raises leg that makes hold and makes maximally strong swing by the leg, and this swing knocks down the adversary's leg.

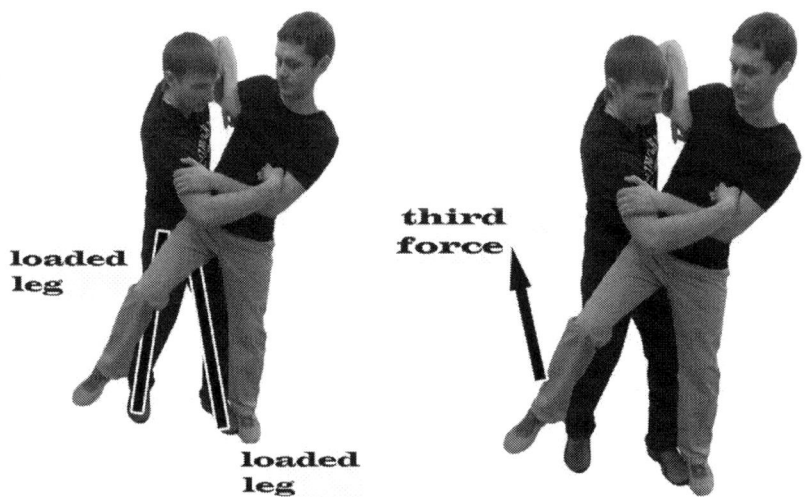

The third stage it is again the additional work by trunk and hands. Hands continue to affect the adversary's structure and to pull forward and down. The trunk a bit bends forward. As a result of three forces action, the adversary's body center goes beyond the foothold area, and adversary loses balance with fall.

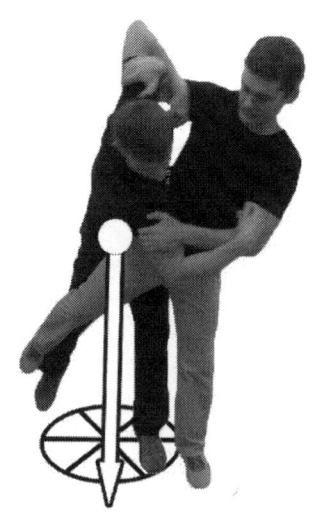

Thus, the general algorithm of any grab-beat may be described in three stages.

1. Preparatory stage – the affect on adversary's structure by hands, the disturbance of balance, the load of adversary's legs with weight or their partial release.

2. Main stage – the strong swing by leg that knocks the adversary's loaded or half-loaded legs (the legs with adversary's body weight) down.

3. Final stage – the additional effect on adversary's structure by hands, the transfer of adversary's weight through the fighter's leg that makes swing.

All three stages are realized together and continuously.

The biomechanics of hooks

The hook it is a hold, at which the effect on adversary's half-loaded or loaded leg by the back side of the fighter's ankle and heel from behind of adversary's leg takes place. The fighter's leg looks like hook, and adversary's leg is as if hooked from behind. Like any hold by legs the hook is preceded by preparatory work by hands to affect the adversary's structure. The aim of this work is to load the leg that the hook is made on with the weight. The release of the leg that the hold is made on from the weight is also practiced at hooks. In this case the hands work at final stage is somewhat different that doesn't change the essence of internal biomechanics of the effect, namely the ability to manage the adversary's body center.

For example, the fighter can load two adversary's legs by hands movement down or he can load the one adversary's leg by the movement of left hand to the left and right one down (see the figure below). It is the first (preparatory) stage of hook execution.

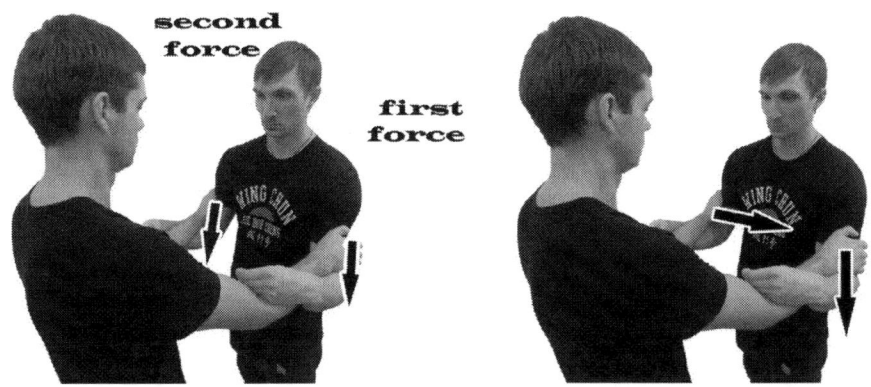

At the second stage of hold the fighter makes preparatory movement by legs for realizing the main effect on adversary's leg by leg (hook) – he raises the right leg from behind of adversary's left leg. The raising of the right leg can be preceded by the step by the left leg forward.

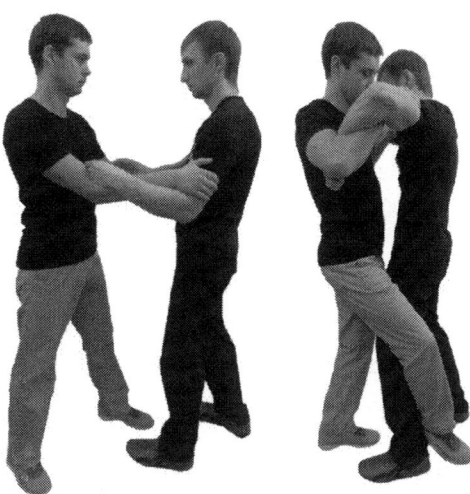

At the final phase of this stage the adversary's left leg remains loaded. The fighter raises leg that makes hold and makes hook as swing by half-bent leg, hooking the adversary's left leg.

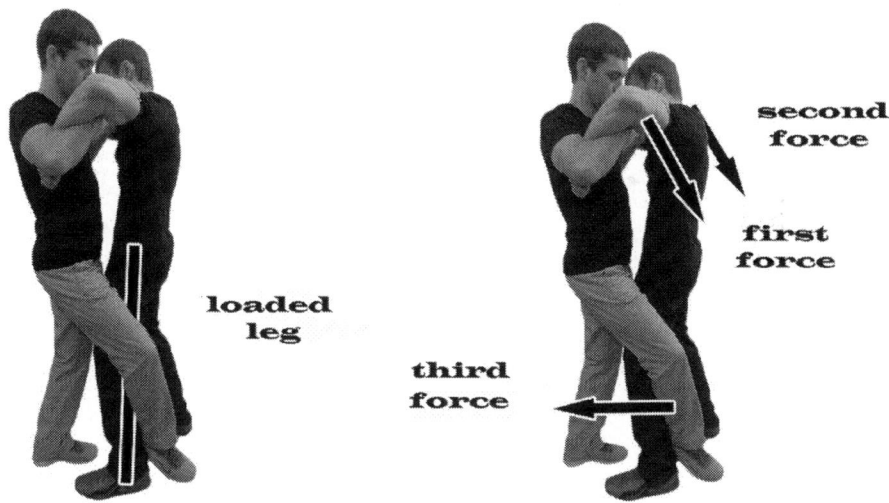

The third stage it is again the additional work by trunk and hands. Hands continue to affect the adversary's structure and to pull back and down. The adversary's trunk a bit bends forward. As a result of three forces action, the adversary's trunk deviates back, the left leg moves forward and adversary's body center goes beyond the foothold area, and adversary loses balance with fall.

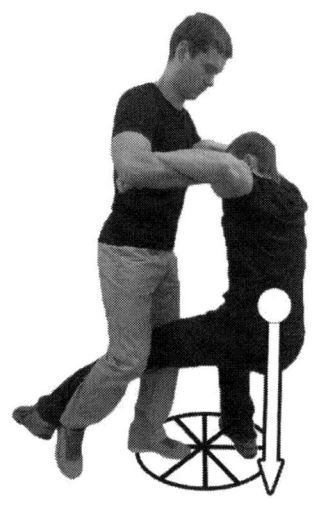

Thus, the general algorithm of any hook may be described in three stages.

1. Preparatory stage – the affect on adversary's structure by hands, the disturbance of balance, the load of leg that the hook will be made on with weight.

2. Main stage – the hook of adversary's leg as swing by the leg that knocks the adversary's loaded leg down and makes it to bend in knee or to move forward.

3. The final stage – the additional affect on adversary's structure by hands as push and pressure back and down, as a result of which the adversary's trunk deviates back.

All three stages are realized together and continuously.

The ankle trips and bridges building

Wing Chun is a striking style, where the blows by hands prevail. To make any ankle trip it is necessary to come into adversary's structure. At that the adversary strikes blows.

That is why to make holds as ankle trips and trips it is very important to be able to make blocks and to build bridges. But only blocks don't allow make the ankle trips. The grips are needed as more complicated bridges building. The ability to make blocks is in the base of grips.

The bridge building it is a technique in Wing Chun that allows to come in contact with adversary's hands and to set contact with adversary's structure through them. There are many applied variants of bridges building as well as bridges themselves.

The bridges can be built using blocks.

The bridges can be built using single grips, the grip of adversary's one hand by the one hand.

Besides the bridges as the simple grips the more complicated grips are possible, for example the double bridges – adversary's one hand by two hands or adversary's two hands by two hands.

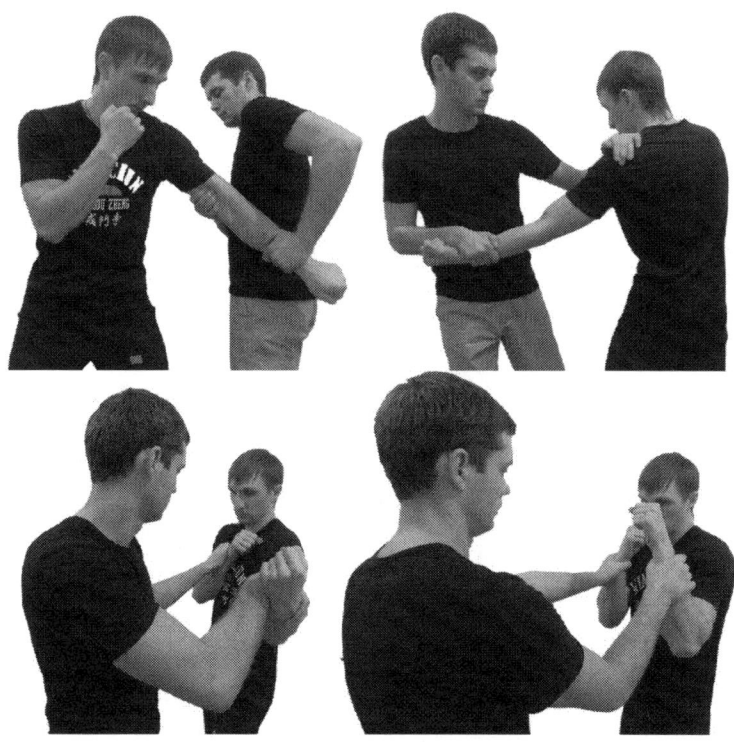

The bridges are also possible as clinch situations.

The bridge building is the one of initial elements of ankle trips technique. By bridges building the fighter comes into adversary's structure and gets a possibility to manage it. If the fighter hasn't mastered the bridges building technique, it becomes practically impossible to make the ankle trip. It determines the importance of bridges building technique for the holds by legs.

The ankle trips and "sticky hands" technique

The work by hands and taking the adversary's structure out of balance are very important at making ankle trips. To make hold it is necessary to manage the adversary's structure and to transfer the adversary's body weight from one leg to the other depending on hold. It is attained by the fighter's preparatory movement and effect on adversary's structure through the contact with adversary's hands. It is a very high skill. It is attained by the sticky hands technique. After building bridge with adversary's striking hand (making block) the fighter begins to manage the adversary's hand (the sticky hands technique) and manages the adversary's structure through it, making adversary to transfer the weight on one or another leg and then makes the necessary ankle trip.

The fighter builds bridge with adversary's hands – sets contact with adversary's hands and then affects the adversary's structure through the contact by pressure, push from himself or jerk on himself. Using the bridges building and "sticky hands" techniques the preparatory stage of hold is realized – the adversary is partially taken out of balance.

Let's give an example. On the first figure the fighter blocks the adversary's striking hand (bridge building). Then the fighter takes the adversary's hand away to the central line by the sticky hands technique and realizes grip – the use of sticky hands technique. Synchronously the fighter makes grip of adversary's neck – building of the second bridge. Using two grips (two bridges), the fighter keeps the adversary with loaded front leg – the control of adversary's structure. The basic Wing Chun techniques – bridges building and "sticky hands" allows fighter to make the ankle trip under adversary's empty (right) leg.

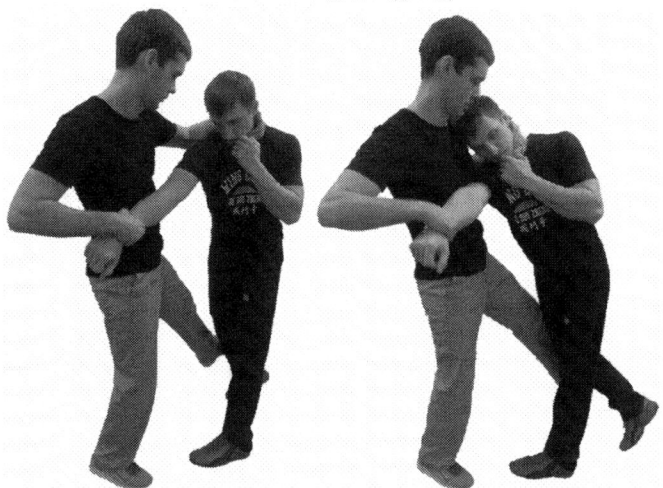

That is why each person, who practices Wing Chun, before beginning the study of ankle trips must master the technique of blows and kicks, blocks, bridges building, grips and sticky hands. All this allows to use and to create the favorable moments for making holds.

The use of adversary's force at ankle trips

At practical execution of ankle trips in free training, for example, in free chi sao or in combat situation, the adversary will manifest his force and resistance. That is why in applied variant the task of each Wing Chun fighter at making ankle trip or trip in stand is to make a good grip, to take the adversary out of balance and to make the ankle trip. Taking into account the fact that the fighter will manifest force, this problem can be solved in different ways.

Three ways are mainly applied:
1. The use of own force;
2. The use of force and inertia of adversary's movement;
3. The use of own force in combination with force and inertia of adversary's movement.

The use of own force only is usually practiced by unskilled fighter or the fighters, who have the evident force advantage over adversary. This way is also typical for hard force styles of martial arts. The evident shortcoming of this way it is, at first, the necessary force and physical advantage over adversary. It makes difficult the use of this way of ankle trips at resistance to the stronger adversary. The second shortcoming is the excessive outlay of own forces that can result in early fatigue. At making ankle trips in this way the fighter must execute all three necessary stages of ankle trip independently at the expanse of own forces – to take out of balance, to undercut the leg and to knock the adversary down by hands.

The example of ankle trip at the expanse of using own force is given on the figures below. At the first stage the fighter takes adversary out of balance by the push diagonally to the right. As a result of push the adversary transfers the body weight on the right leg – the loaded one, at that the left leg is released from the weight – empty leg. At the second stage the fighter undercuts the adversary's left empty leg by the right one, depriving him of support. At the third stage the fighter uses the own force of hands and trunk and pulls the adversary to the right on the undercut leg. The adversary can't lean on undercut leg, loses balance under the own weight and falls. At all three stages the fighter used the own force.

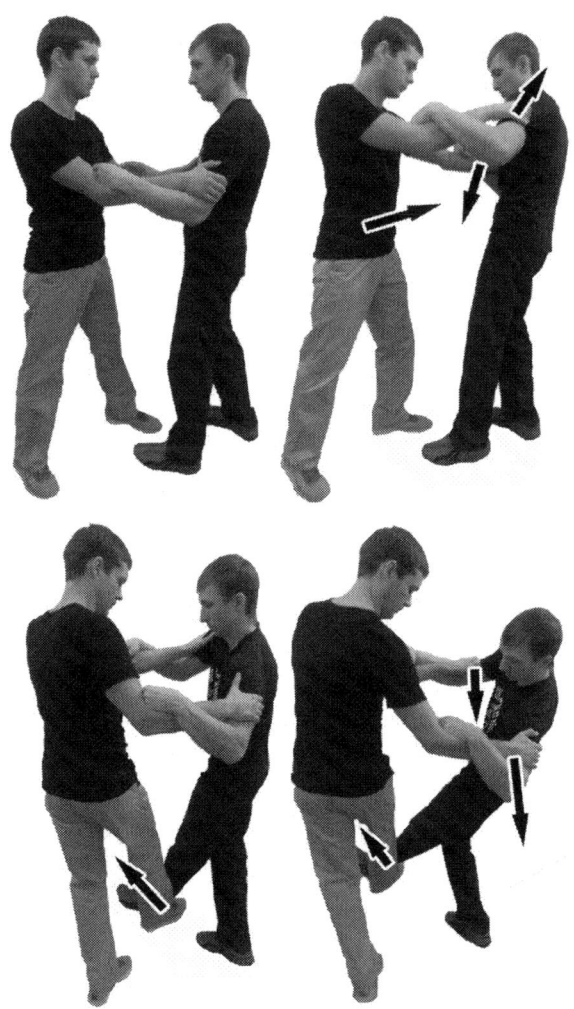

The use of adversary's force and inertia is practiced by the masters and based on counterattacks and use of adversary's mistakes. This way is also typical for the soft styles of martial arts. Its advantage is in fact that the fighter practically doesn't spend the own forces. And the use of adversary's force gives to physically weaker fighter a possibility to resist the stronger adversary. This way needs great attention, experience and mastership from the fighter. The use of this way is most effective against the unskilled adversaries, who don't observe the principles of centrality and rooting at blows, so, come out of balance themselves, facilitating the ankle trip for the fighter. At executing ankle trips in this way the adversary realizes the first stage independently – takes himself out of balance. The fighter must be attentive to realize two following stages in proper time – to undercut the leg and to knock the adversary down by hands. The shortcoming of this way is in fact that it is difficult to apply it against the skilled adversaries, who use counterattacking style of conducting combat themselves and observe the principles of centrality and rooting at the attacks.

The example of ankle trip at the expanse of using the adversary's force is given on the figures below. The adversary makes step by the left leg forward and strikes blow by the left hand. As a result of blow and step forward, the body weight is unevenly distributed between legs, legs are put broadly and the stand steadiness is broken. In fact the adversary breaks the own balance independently at the expanse of own blow force that is realizes the first stage by his own. The fighter makes step by the right leg forward and makes deviation from blow to the right, bringing the adversary down. Then the fighter makes jump with the change of stand – the right leg is forward, the left one – back. Using the force and inertia, appeared at the change of stand, the fighter undercuts the adversary's front leg – the second stage. The adversary can resist the ankle trip, because his legs are put broadly as a result of blow and bringing down, and loses balance with fall – the third stage. The fighter used the own force only at the second stage. At the first and third ones he used the adversary's force and unsteadiness.

The fighters, who use the first two ways can succeed in isolated cases, but the experience testifies that the best way is the third one, when fighter uses the force and inertia of adversary's movement, applying the own forces in the same direction if necessary. It allows easily take the adversary out of balance and forces him to make movement in opposite direction with big force for keeping steadiness.

The example of ankle trip at the expanse of using the adversary's force and addition of own one is given on the figures below. The adversary strikes blow by the right hand. At this he essentially transfers the weight on the front leg. As a result of blow the body weight is distributed between legs unevenly, the most part of it is on the left front leg – loaded leg. The weight is insignificantly distributed on the right back leg – empty leg, the stand steadiness is broken. In fact the adversary breaks the own balance independently at the expanse of own blow force that is he realizes the first stage by his own. The fighter makes step by the left leg to the left and makes deviation from blow to the left, synchronously with block by the right forearm. Block is realized softly and redirects the adversary's force forward and down. The block force is added to the adversary's blow one and acts in the same direction. At once after block the fighter makes grip of adversary's striking hand by the right one and grip of adversary's neck by the left one, redirecting the blow force to the right and down. At the expanse of these actions the fighter transfers more of adversary's weight on his right leg and breaks his steadiness. Then the fighter undercuts the adversary's empty back leg by the left leg – the second stage. At once after ankle trip, the fighter makes the jerk of grip on himself without interruption – the third stage. At the expanse of the fact that the support of back leg is absent, the adversary loses balance because of his body gravity force. The fighter used the adversary's force at the first stage, added the own force at the second and third ones.

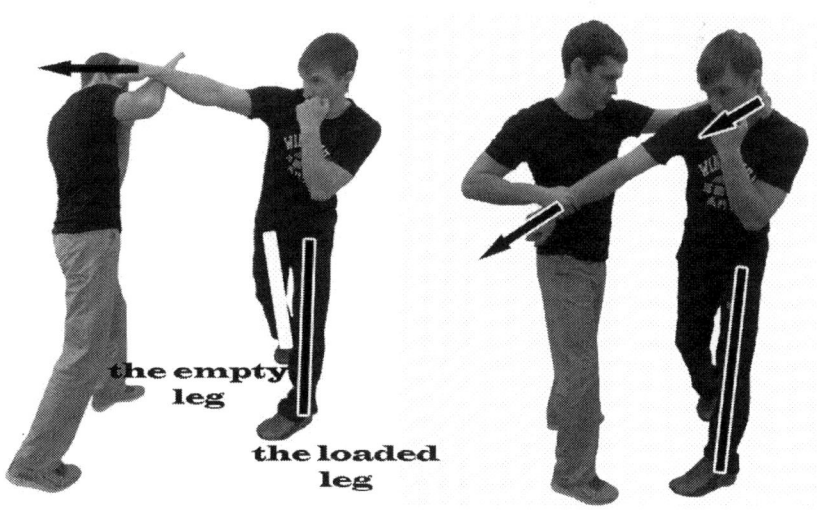

Thus all holds by legs in Wing Chun are realized either as a development of adversary's movement or using his resistance. The use of adversary's force, movement inertia and body weight essentially facilitates the hold execution. The different ways of disturbance of adversary's balance can be used in all eight main directions.

THE SIDE ANKLE TRIP

Basic variant

The practicing persons stand in front of each other in side stands and elbow grips. The fighter forces partner to transfer the body weight on the back right leg by hands push in grip. The partner's front (left) leg is released from weight. The fighter undercuts the empty (left) leg by the right foot and makes jerk of the partner to the right-down by both hands. The partner falls, because the support of the left leg is absent that is undercut.

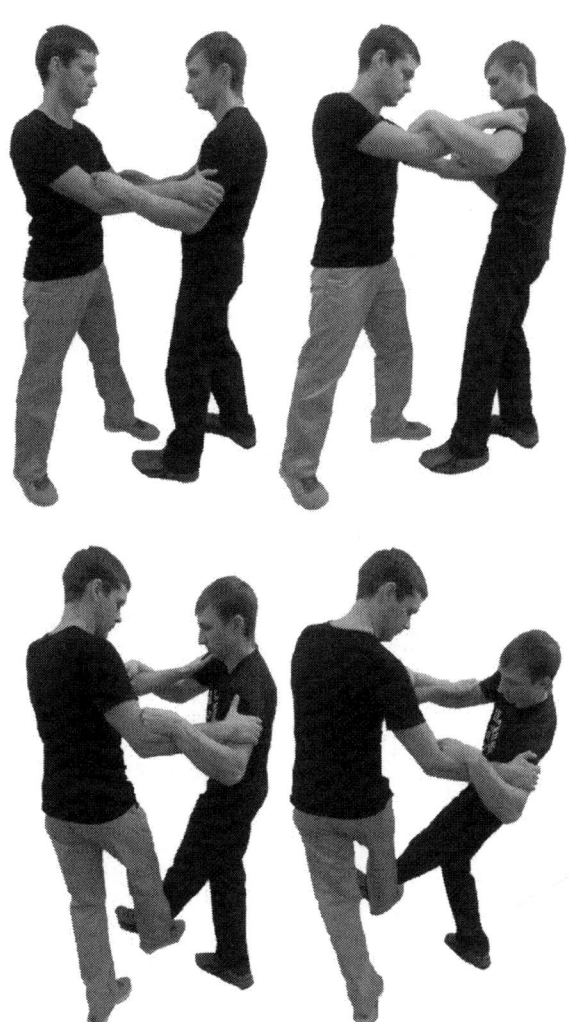

This ankle trip can be made in attacking variant. The adversaries are in right-side stands (left hand forward, right one behind). The fighter makes step to the right-forward by the left leg, turning toe to the right. Then he takes the right leg forward, changing stands. The right leg undercuts the adversary's front (left) leg at the expanse of inertia of step and turn.

This variant of ankle trip can be also realized as counterattacking one. The adversary strikes blow by the left hand. Fighter makes step to the right and forward by the right leg, synchronously deviating from the blow to the right. Then he puts the left leg to the right one fast (possibly in jump) and skips to the left leg, synchronously taking the right one forward behind the adversary's front (left) leg. The fighter undercuts the adversary's front left leg by the right one at the expanse of gathered inertia.

The same variant of ankle trip can be realized in attacking variant by building bridges by hands. The adversaries are in right-side stands (left hand forward, right one behind). The fighter makes step forward by the left leg, covers and catches the adversary's front left hand by the left one. Synchronously the right leg is taken forward, and left hand presses on adversary's hand and on the structure through it. It makes adversary to transfer the body weight on the back (right) leg. The right leg undercuts the adversary's front (left) leg at the expanse of inertia of step and turn. Synchronously the fighter's right hand hooks the adversary's right shoulder by the hand hook (mantis paw) and makes jerk down.

The same variant of ankle trip can be realized with building bridges and striking blows by hands. The fighter makes step forward by the left leg, he covers and catches the adversary's front left hand by his left hand. Synchronously the right leg is taken forward, and left hand strikes blow by the forearm in adversary's head above his caught hand. It forces the adversary to transfer weight on the right leg. At blow the left hand continues to hold the adversary's hand and to pull him on the fighter. The right leg undercuts the adversary's front (left) leg at the expanse of inertia of step and turn, and the right hand presses on adversary's head down.

This variant of ankle trip can be realized as counterattacking one with building bridges. The adversary strikes blow by the left hand. Fighter makes step to the right and forward by the right leg, synchronously deviates and makes block by the left forearm with further grip of adversary's striking hand. Then, keeping the adversary's hand and realizing the jerk of adversary's structure on himself, fighter skips to the left leg, synchronously taking the right one forward, putting it behind the adversary's front leg. The blow is stricken synchronously in adversary's head by the right forearm. At the expanse of blow the adversary transfers weight on the back leg, and the fighter undercuts the adversary's front leg by the right one.

The hold can be made analogously, if the fighter's right hand doesn't strike blow by forearm above the adversary's hand, but catches his right hand under the left one.

The adversaries are in right-side stands. The fighter makes step forward by the right leg and makes the internal bridge by the right hand, makes the snake block, passing along the adversary's central line between his hands and bringing the adversary's left hand from internal side down to the left. In the end of bridge he catches his left shoulder. At that the fighter's right forearm presses on adversary's hand, forcing to transfer weight of adversary's back knee. The adversary's left leg is partially released from load. At once after grip the right leg undercuts the adversary's front (left) leg, and the right hand makes jerk of adversary's structure down.

The adversaries are in right-side stands. The fighter makes step forward by the left leg and makes grip of adversary's left hand by the right hand from external side. Then the fighter takes the right hand forward and synchronously covers the adversary's hand by own right elbow, forming the lever. The right leg undercuts the adversary's front (left) leg at the expanse of inertia of step and turn, and the right hand presses the adversary's structure by elbow through the adversary's hand.

The adversaries are in right-side stands. The fighter makes step forward by the left leg and catches both adversary's forearms by hands as it is shown on the figure. Then the fighter takes the right leg forward. The right leg undercuts the adversary's front (left) one at the expanse of inertia of step and turn, and the fighter's hand in grip realizes the jerk of adversary's structure to the right and down.

THE ANKLE TRIP FROM INSIDE

Basic variant

The practicing persons stand in front of each other in side stands and elbow grips. The fighter transfers weight on the front left leg, at that he forces the adversary's structure by elbow grip to transfer weight on the right back leg. Then he makes sub-step by the right leg and takes the left one behind the adversary's front left leg from inside, hooking it by the foot and shin. The adversary's structure is undercut with fall at the expanse of swing by the left leg back and push by hands in elbow grip back.

The ankle trip can be realized in attacking variant. The adversaries are in right-side stands (left hand forward, right one behind). The fighter makes step forward and to the right by the right leg, coming close to adversary. Then the left leg makes ankle trip from internal side of adversary's front left leg. The left leg undercuts the adversary's front (left) leg from inside at the expanse of inertia of step and swing.

The ankle trip can be made in attacking variant with building bridges. The fighter makes step to the right-forward by the right leg and builds the bridge by the left forearm on adversary's left hand, then at once makes grip and jerk on himself. Synchronously with jerk the fighter undercuts the adversary's front leg from inside by the left leg. The adversary loses balance at the expanse of two forces of jerk by hands and ankle trip by leg.

This combination can be made analogously in counterattacking variant. The adversary strikes blow by the left hand. Fighter makes step to the right-forward by the right leg, deviates from blow, makes block by the left forearm from external side of adversary's striking hand and at once makes grip and jerk on himself. Synchronously with jerk the fighter undercuts the adversary's front leg from inside by the left leg. The adversary loses balance at the expanse of two force of jerk by hand and ankle trip by leg.

The adversaries are in right-side stands. The fighter makes step forward by the left leg. His right and left hands pass along the adversary's central line. The right hand builds the bridge from internal side of adversary's striking hand, making grip of elbow and shoulder. Left hand covers the adversary's left shoulder. Then the fighter pulls the right leg and takes the left one forward by jump from inside of adversary's front left leg. Then the fighter undercuts the adversary's left leg by the abrupt movement of the left leg back. Fighter's hands, being in grip with adversary's shoulder and elbow, press down, so the adversary's structure is undercut.

The grip of elbow and shoulder is rather strong and firm grip that allows control and affect the adversary's structure more confidently. But the grip of elbow it is a deep grip that needs rapprochement with adversary that is a threat of blow. That is why the grip can be also realized with the shoulder of adversary's front hand as it is shown on the figure below. In other details the hold is realized according to aforesaid mechanics.

The analogous combination can be realized in counterattacking variant. The adversary strikes blow by the left hand. Fighter makes step forward and to the left by the left leg, deviates to the left and makes block by the right forearm from inside of striking hand. At once after block fighter catches the adversary's hand and takes it to his right side. Left hand covers the adversary's left shoulder. Then the fighter pulls the right leg and takes the left leg forward from inside of adversary's left front leg by jump. Then the fighter undercuts the adversary's left leg by the abrupt movement of left leg back. Fighter's hands, being in grip with adversary's shoulder and hand, press down, so the adversary's structure is undercut.

The adversaries are in right-side stands. The fighter makes step forward by the left leg. The right hand is laid on adversary's left one, making grip. Left hand covers the adversary's left shoulder. Then the fighter pulls the right leg and takes the left leg forward from inside of adversary's left front leg by jump. Then the fighter undercuts the adversary's left leg by the abrupt movement of left leg back. Fighter's hands, being in grip with adversary's shoulder and hand, press down, so the adversary's structure is undercut.

The adversaries are in right-side stands. The fighter makes step forward by the left leg and makes grip of adversary's hands by both hands as it is shown on the figure. Keeping the grip firmly, the fighter makes sub-step by the right leg and synchronously takes the left leg behind the adversary's left one from inside. This movement by legs can be made as a jump. Then the fighter undercuts the adversary's left leg by the abrupt movement of the left leg back. The fighter's hands in grip push forward-down, so the adversary's structure is undercut.

The adversaries are in right-side stands. The fighter makes step forward by the left leg and builds the bridge with adversary's left hand by his left hand. Then he catches the adversary's left wrist by the left hand and adversary's left elbow by his right hand. The fighter is as if pulled closer to adversary by created grip and takes the left leg from inside and behind of adversary's front leg. Left hand is released from the grip and realizes the blow-pressure by palm in adversary's left shoulder as it is shown on the figure. Right hand keeps the adversary's elbow in grip. At the moment of blow on adversary's shoulder by the left hand, the fighter's left leg undercuts the adversary's left one. The adversary's structure is undercut at the expanse of two multidirectional force vectors.

The adversaries are in right-side stands. The adversary strikes blow by the right hand. Fighter makes step forward and to the left by the left leg, deviates to the left and blocks the adversary's hand by the right forearm from external side of striking hand. At once after block by the technique of sticky hands the fighter makes grip of adversary's hand as it is shown on the figure. At that the left hand is laid on the shoulder of adversary's striking hand for more firm control. Synchronously with grip the left leg is taken forward between the adversary's legs and hooks the adversary's front left leg from inside. Then the fighter undercuts the adversary's front left leg from inside by the abrupt movement of right leg towards himself. Fighter's hands push forward-down at grip, so the adversary's structure is undercut.

THE FRONT ANKLE TRIP
Basic variant

The practicing persons stand in front of each other in side stands and elbow grips. The fighter makes jerk of adversary's structure on himself and to the left. The adversary transfers weight on the left front leg, right leg is without weight – empty. Synchronously with jerk the fighter raises the left leg and undercuts the adversary's right leg by the swing, without giving it a possibility to make step forward and restore balance. Then the fighter turns trunk to the left and makes throw, continuing to pull the adversary on himself. The partner falls, because the support of left leg is absent that is undercut. For strengthening the undercutting force the fighter can preliminary make step forward and to the right by the right leg together with the first jerk on himself, putting the right leg on the same line from external side of the partner's left leg. So, the twisting and undercutting force will be stronger.

The adversaries are in right-side stands. The adversary strikes blow by the right hand. Fighter makes step forward and to the left by the left leg, deviates to the left and blocks the adversary's hand by the right forearm from external side of striking hand. At once after block through the technique of sticky hands, the fighter makes grip of adversary's hand as it is shown on the figure. At that the left hand strikes blow in adversary's nape by the open palm and makes grip of neck. The double grip is made. The fighter makes jerk of adversary's structure on himself. At that the fighter transfers the body weight on his right leg. Synchronously with jerk the fighter undercuts the adversary's right leg by the swing of his left one. Hands in grip continue to pull the adversary's structure forward and down. The adversary loses balance with fall at the expanse of synchronism of hands force application and ankle trip by the leg.

THE BACK ANKLE TRIP BY KICK
Basic variant

The practicing persons stand in front of each other in side stands and elbow grips. The fighter makes step to the right and forward by the right leg and synchronously makes jerk of adversary's structure to the right. Adversary transfers the body weight on the left front leg. At once after that the fighter raises the left leg, bent in knee behind the partner's left leg. Then fighter strikes kick in the partner's front knee bend by the left leg, and synchronously he realizes push and pressure back-down by hands in elbow grip.

This hold can be analogously executed with kick-ankle trip by other leg. For that the fighter makes step to the right by the left leg and synchronously makes jerk of adversary's structure to the right. Adversary transfers the weight on the left front leg. At once after that the fighter raises right leg, bent in knee, behind the partner's left front leg. Then the fighter strikes kick in adversary's front knee bend by the right leg, and synchronously hands in elbow grip make push and pressure back-down.

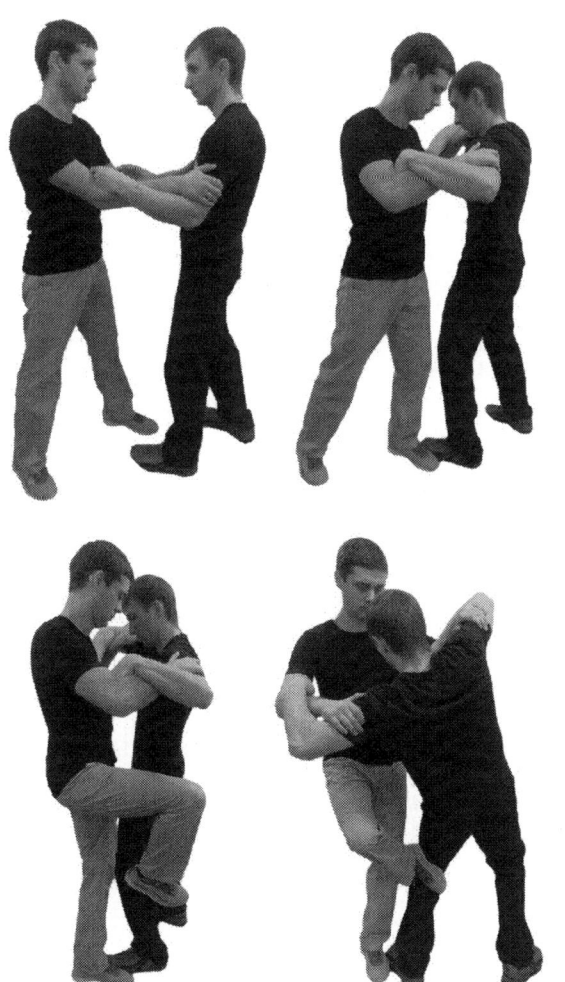

The adversaries are in right-side stands. The adversary strikes blow by the left hand. Fighter makes step forward and to the right by the right leg, deviates and synchronously makes block by the left hand. At once after block the fighter catches the adversary's left forearm and makes jerk of adversary's structure on himself. Synchronously the fighter's left leg, bent in knee, is raised behind the adversary's left front leg. Then the fighter makes kick in the partner's front knee bend by the left leg.

The adversaries are in right-side stands. The adversary strikes blow by the left hand. Fighter makes step forward and to the right by the right leg, deviates and synchronously makes block by the left forearm from external side. At once after block through the technique of sticky hands, the fighter makes grip of adversary's hand and realizes the jerk of adversary's structure on himself as it is shown on the figure. At that the right hand is laid on the shoulder of adversary's striking hand for more firm control. Synchronously with grip the left leg is put to the right one, at once after that the right leg, bent in knee, is raised behind the adversary's left front leg. Then the fighter strikes kick in adversary's front knee bend by the right leg, and synchronously hands in elbow grip realize the pressure back-down.

THE BACK TRIP

Basic variant

The practicing persons stand in front of each other in side stands and elbow grips. Fighter makes step to the right and forward by the right leg and synchronously makes jerk of adversary's structure to the right. Adversary transfers weight on the left front leg. At once after that the fighter raises left leg behind the partner's left front leg. Then the fighter makes swing back and undercuts the adversary's front leg. Synchronously hands in elbow grip realize push and pressure back-down. The partner falls, because the support of the left leg is absent that is undercut.

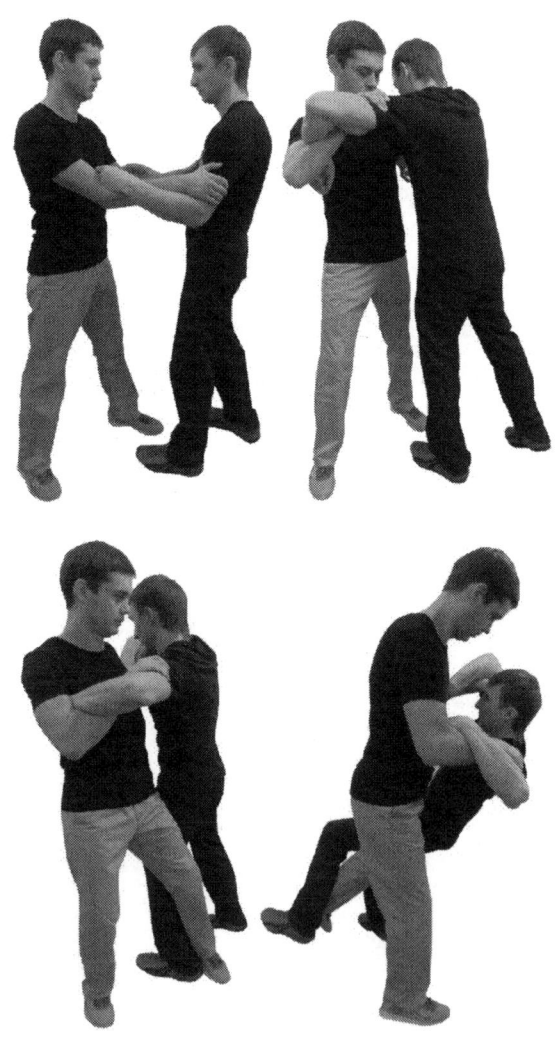

The adversaries are in right-side stands. The fighter makes step forward to the right by the right leg. Synchronously the right hand builds external bridge on adversary's left hand, making grip, and the left one passes along the adversary's central line between his hands and covers the adversary's left shoulder. As a result, the adversary's left hand is closely pressed to the fighter's left shoulder. Then the fighter takes the right leg forward behind the adversary's left front leg. Then he undercuts the adversary's left leg by the abrupt movement of the left leg back. Fighter's left hand presses back and down on adversary's shoulder, so the adversary's structure is undercut.

If the adversary stands far and fighter can't make grip of his shoulder by the left hand, the left hand is laid on adversary's left elbow as it is shown on the figure below. Then the trip is made as it is described above.

The other variant of grip in this hold is the overlap of the left hand on adversary's neck. At that the adversary's left hand is pressed closely to adversary's trunk by the right one. Then the trip is made as it is described above. At the moment of trip the left hand presses on neck to the right and down, so the adversary falls.

The adversaries are in right-side stands. The fighter makes step forward-to the right by the right leg. Synchronously the right hand builds the internal bridge on adversary's left hand, making grip from internal side and extending it on himself, and the left hand builds bridge on adversary's right hand, making its grip from external side and pressing it to adversary's trunk. Then the fighter takes the right leg forward behind the adversary's front left leg. Then he beats the adversary's left leg by the abrupt movement of left leg back. Fighter's left hand presses on adversary's structure through the grip back and down, so the adversary's structure is undercut.

The adversaries are in right-side stands. The fighter's right hand passes along the adversary's central line and builds the bridge from internal side of adversary's left hand, making grip of his elbow. Left hand covers the adversary's left shoulder. Then the fighter takes the left leg forward behind the adversary's front left leg. Then the fighter beats the adversary's left leg by the abrupt movement of his left leg back. Fighter's left hand on adversary's shoulder presses back and down, his right hand keeps the adversary's left hand in grip, so the adversary's structure is undercut.

The grip of elbow and shoulder is rather strong and firm and allows control the adversary's structure and affect on it more confidently. But the grip of elbow is a deeper one that needs rapprochement with adversary that is a threat of blow. That is why the grip can be made also with forearm of adversary front hand as it is shown on the figure below. In other respects the hold is realized according to aforesaid mechanics.

The adversaries are in right-side stands. The fighter makes step forward by the left leg and builds the bridge with adversary's left hand as a grip from external side by the left hand. And his right hand catches the adversary's left shoulder. The jerk of adversary's structure on himself is made by created grip. When the adversary makes movement forward under effect of jerk, the fighter takes his left leg forward behind the adversary's left front leg. Left hand is released from the grip and strikes blow by forearm in adversary's head. Right hand keeps the adversary's elbow in grip. At the moment of blow by hand the fighter's left leg undercuts the adversary's left one. The adversary's structure is undercut at the expanse of two multidirectional force vectors.

The adversaries are in right-side stands. The fighter makes step forward by the left leg and builds the bridge with adversary's left hand by the grip of wrist by the left hand. The jerk of adversary's structure on himself is realized through created grip. When the adversary makes the movement forward under effect of jerk, the fighter takes his left leg forward behind the adversary's left front leg. Left hand is released from the grip and strikes blow by forearm in adversary's trunk, neck or head. At the moment of blow by hand the fighter's left leg undercuts the adversary's left one. The adversary's structure is undercut at the expanse of two multidirectional force vectors.

The adversaries are in right-side stands. The adversary strikes blow by the right hand. Fighter makes step to the left by the left leg with synchronous block by the right forearm. In the contact point fighter manages the adversary's structure by the "sticky hands" technique and redirect the adversary's blow forward and down. When the adversary makes movement forward, the fighter takes his right leg forward behind the adversary's right leg. Right forearm strikes blow in adversary's trunk, neck or head. At the moment of blow by hand the fighter's right leg undercuts the adversary's right one.

In this hold the fighter can also lay the left hand on shoulder, pressing down or on adversary's spine, pressing the lumbar flexure that strengthens the trip.

The adversaries are in right-side stands. The adversary makes blow by the right hand. Fighter makes step to the left by the left leg with synchronous block by the left palm. In the contact point fighter manages the adversary's structure through the technique of "sticky hands" and redirects the adversary's blow forward, at that the right hand passes along the adversary's striking one. When adversary makes movement forward, the fighter makes grip of the elbow bend of adversary's striking hand by the right hand, striking abrupt blow on it. Right leg is taken forward behind the adversary's right leg and undercuts it by the swing back. At that the left hand in grip presses the adversary's structure down.

THE FRONT TRIP

Basic variant

The practicing persons stand in front of each other in side stands and elbow grips. The fighter makes step to the right and forward by the right leg behind his front leg (cross step) and makes jerk of adversary's structure on himself and to the right. As a result of this movement the fighter turns to the right and crosses legs. Then he puts the left leg in front of adversary's left one practically at the same line, at that he turns spine to the adversary. Then the fighter makes trip to adversary at the expanse of abrupt beat of the left leg by knee bend and pull of adversary's structure by hands forward and down.

The front trip can be made also under adversary's right leg. In this case the fighter makes jerk of adversary's structure on himself and to the left. Adversary transfers the weight on toes. Synchronously with jerk the fighter makes step forward by the right leg. Then he makes cross step and puts the left leg behind his right one, near the partner's left front leg. Then he puts the right leg under the partner's right one. Then the fighter makes beat of the partner's right leg by the right knee bend with synchronous pull of partner by hands forward and down, making throw.

The adversaries are in right-side stands. Fighter makes step by the left leg. His right hand passes along the adversary's central line and builds the bridge from internal side of adversary's left hand, making grip of forearm. Then the fighter makes cross step by the right leg forward behind his left leg, trying to put it as close to the adversary as possible. At that the left hand covers the adversary's neck from the left side. Then the fighter takes the left leg forward in front of adversary's front left leg. Then the fighter undercuts the adversary's left leg by the abrupt movement of the left leg back. Fighter's hands in the grip with adversary's elbow and neck pull forward and down, so the adversary's structure is undercut.

The same hold can be made in counterattacking variant. The adversaries are in right-side stands. Adversary strikes blow by the left hand. Fighter makes step forward and to the left by the left leg, deviates to the left and blocks the adversary's hand by the right forearm from inside. At once after block through the technique of sticky hands the fighter makes grip of adversary's hand. At that the left hand is laid on adversary's right one and catches it. Synchronously the right leg makes sub-step to the left one. And at once the left leg is put in front of adversary's left leg practically at the same line. At that the fighter turns spine to adversary. Then he makes trip to adversary at the expanse of abrupt beat of the left leg by knee and pull of adversary's structure forward and down by hands.

The adversaries are in right-side stands. Adversary strikes blow by the right hand. The fighter makes step forward by the left leg, deviates to the left and blocks the adversary's hand by the right forearm from external side of the striking hand. At once after block through the technique of sticky hands the fighter makes grip of adversary's hand as it is shown on the figure. At that the left hand is laid on the shoulder of adversary's striking hand for more firm control. Synchronously with grip the right leg makes sub-step to the left one. And at once the left leg is put in front of adversary's left front leg practically at the same line. At that the fighter turns spine to adversary. Then he makes throw of adversary at the expanse of abrupt beat of the left leg by knee (or swing by the left leg back) and pull of adversary's structure forward and down by hands.

THE GRAB

Basic variant

The fighter makes jerk of adversary's structure on himself and to the left. Adversary transfers the weight on toes. Synchronously with jerk the fighter makes step forward by the right leg. Then the fighter makes cross step and puts the left leg behind his right one, near the partner's left front leg. At that the fighter turns spine to adversary. Then he makes swing by the right leg and beats the adversary's right leg, and hand continue to pull forward and down.

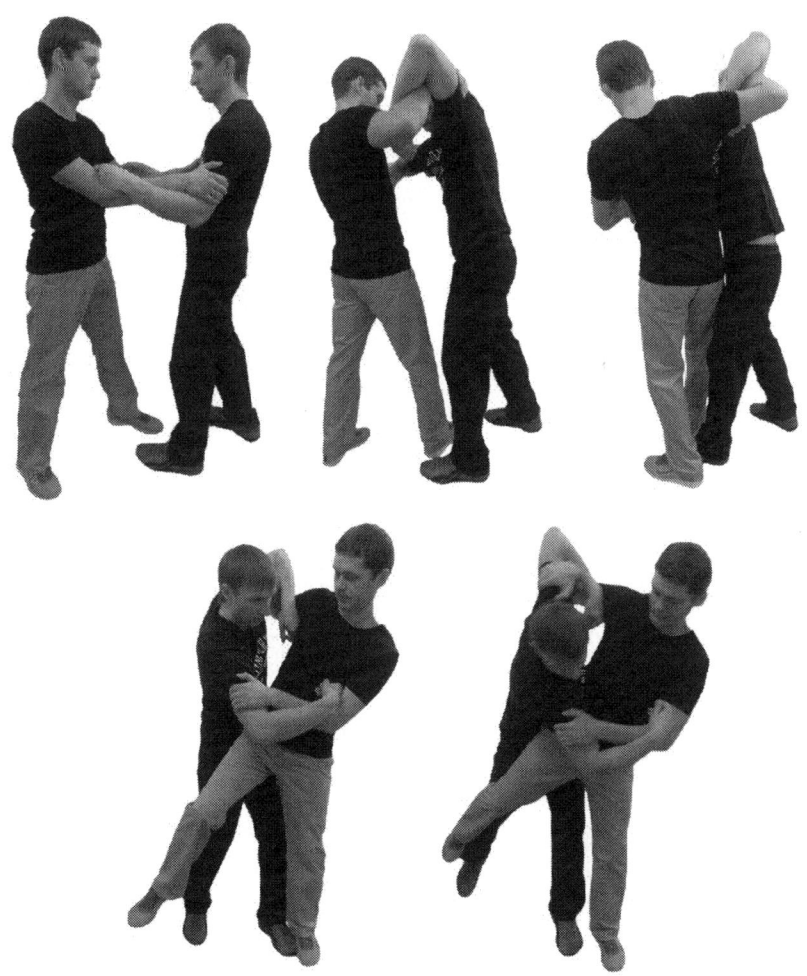

The other variant of hold can be the beat of partner's left leg instead of the right one. In this case at final stage the fighter puts his right leg in front of adversary's right one and makes amplitude swing back, undercutting the adversary's left leg with synchronous pull of the partner forward and down by hands, making throw.

The fighter also can come into adversary's structure from the left leg. He makes jerk of adversary's structure forward and to the left, transferring the body weight on his left leg. Right leg makes sub-step to the left one. And at once the left leg is taken in front of adversary's left one. At that the fighter turns spine to adversary. Then the adversary's leg is beaten at the expanse of abrupt swing by the leg back. Fighter's hands pull the adversary's structure forward and down.

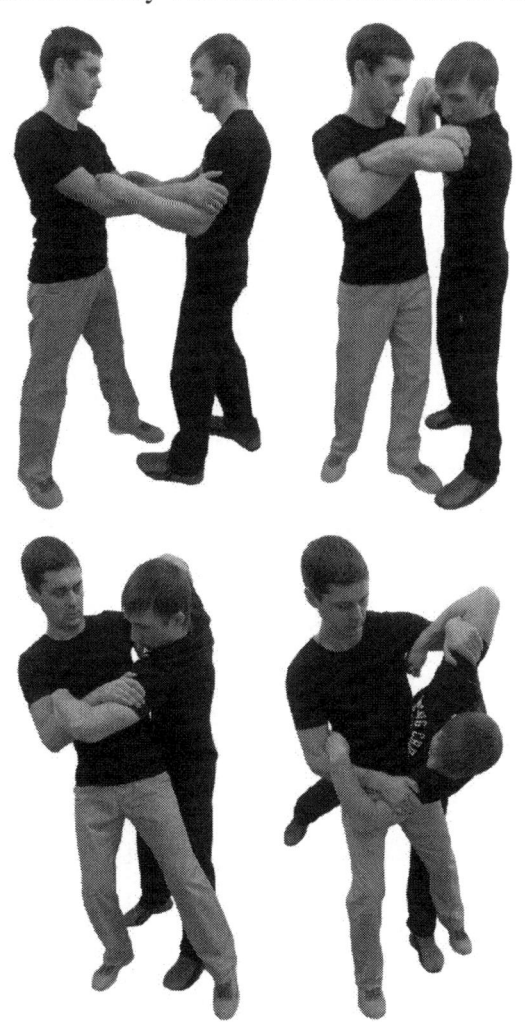

The adversaries are in right-side stands. Adversary strikes blow by the left hand. The fighter makes step forward by the right leg and blocks the adversary's hand by the left forearm. At once after block through the technique of sticky hands the fighter makes grip of adversary's hand and jerk of adversary's structure on himself as it is shown on the figure. Then he makes sub-step by the left leg to the right one and turns spine to adversary. Then he makes abrupt swing back by the right leg, beats the adversary's left leg from inside and up. Fighter's hands in grip push forward-down, so the adversary's structure is undercut.

The adversaries are in right-side stands. Adversary strikes blow by the left hand. Fighter makes step forward by the right leg and blocks the adversary's hand by the left forearm. At once after block through the technique of sticky hands fighter makes grip of adversary's hand and jerk of adversary's structure on himself as it is shown on the figure. At that the right hand is laid on the shoulder of adversary's striking hand for more firm control. Synchronously with grip the right leg is taken in front of the adversary's left front leg. Then the fighter beats the adversary's left leg out by the abrupt movement of right leg back. Fighter's hands in grip push forward-down, so the adversary's structure is undercut.

The adversaries are in right-side stands. Adversary strikes blow by the left hand. The fighter makes step forward by the right leg and blocks the adversary's hand by the left forearm from inside. At once after block through the technique of sticky hands fighter makes grip of adversary's hand and jerk of adversary's structure on himself as it is shown on the figure. Together with jerk the fighter makes sub-step by the left leg to the right one, turns spine to adversary, right leg is near the adversary's right one. At that fighter's right hand passes under adversary's striking one, making grip of the shoulder from below as it is shown on the figure. Then the fighter makes abrupt swing back by the right leg, beats the adversary's right leg up. Fighter's hands in grip push forward-down, so the adversary's structure is undercut.

THE EXTERNAL HOOK

Basic variant

The practicing persons are in front of each other in side stands and elbow grips. Fighter transfers the weight on the front left leg and takes right one behind the adversary's left front leg. The adversary's structure is undercut with fall at the expanse of swing by the right leg back and push by hands in elbow grip back.

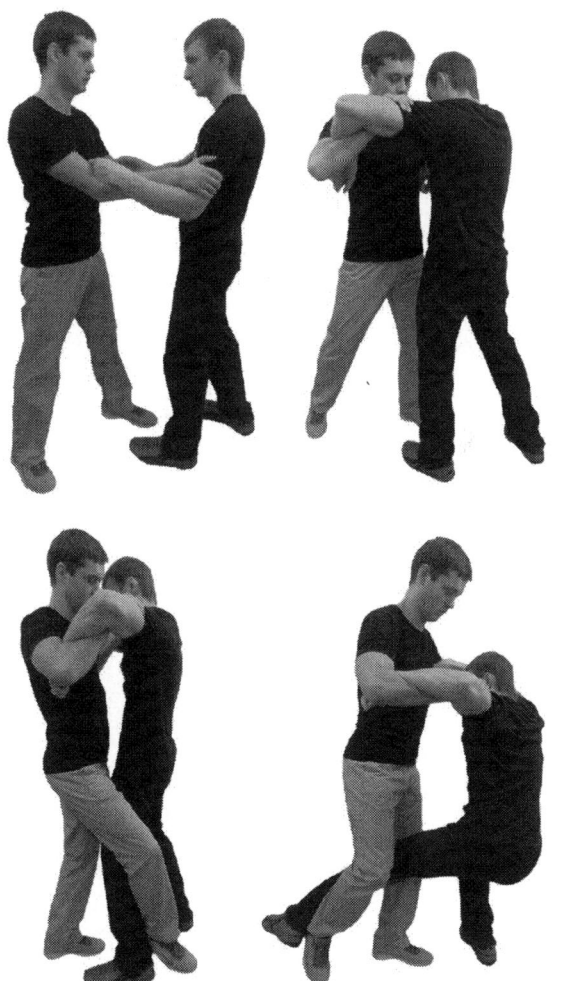

The adversaries are in right-side stands. The fighter makes step forward by the left leg. His left hand passes along the adversary's central line and builds the bridge from internal side of adversary's left hand, making the grip of elbow. Left hand covers the adversary's left shoulder. Then fighter takes the right leg forward behind the adversary's left front leg. Then he hooks the adversary's left leg by the abrupt movement of right leg back. Fighter's hands in grip with adversary's shoulder and elbow press down, so the adversary's structure is undercut.

The grip of elbow and shoulder is rather strong and firm and allows control the adversary's structure and affect it more confidently. But the grip of elbow is deeper and needs come closer to adversary that is a threat of blow. That is why the grip can be realized also with forearm of adversary's front hand as it is shown on the figure below. In other respects this hold is realized according to aforesaid technique.

The adversaries are in right-side stands. Fighter makes step forward by the left leg and makes clinch grip of adversary's neck by both hands. Synchronously with grip the right leg is taken forward behind the adversary's front left leg. Then fighter hooks the adversary's left leg by the abrupt movement of right leg back. Fighter's hands in grip with neck press forward-down, so the adversary's structure is undercut.

The adversaries are in right-side stands. Fighter makes step forward by the left leg and makes grip of adversary's hands by both hands as it is shown on the figure. Synchronously with grip the right leg is taken forward behind the adversary's left front leg. Then fighter hooks the adversary's left leg by the abrupt movement of right leg back. Fighter's hands in grip press forward-down, so the adversary's structure is undercut.

The adversaries are in right-side stands. The adversary strikes blow by the left hand. Fighter makes step forward by the left leg and blocks the adversary's hand. At once after block through the technique of sticky hands the fighter makes grip of adversary's hand and jerk of adversary's structure on himself as it is shown on the figure. At that the right hand is laid on the shoulder of adversary's striking hand for more firm control. Synchronously with grip the right leg is taken forward behind the adversary's left front leg. Then fighter hooks the adversary's left leg by the abrupt movement of right leg back. Fighter's hands in grip press forward-down, so the adversary's structure is undercut.

The adversaries are in right-side stands. The adversary strikes blow by the right hand. Fighter makes step forward and to the left by the left leg and blocks the adversary's hand by the right forearm. At once after block through the technique of sticky hands the fighter makes grip of adversary's hand and jerk of adversary's structure on himself as it is shown on the figure. At that the left hand is laid on the shoulder of adversary's striking hand for more firm control. Synchronously with grip the right leg is taken forward behind the adversary's left front leg. Then fighter hooks the adversary's left leg by the abrupt movement of right leg back. Fighter's hands in grip press forward-down, so the adversary's structure is undercut.

The adversaries are in right-side stands. The adversary strikes blow by the right hand. Fighter makes step forward and to the left by the left leg and blocks the adversary's hand by the right forearm. At once after block through the technique of sticky hands the fighter makes grip of adversary's hand and lays the left hand on adversary's neck. At that the fighter's weight is transferred on the right leg. Left leg is taken forward behind the adversary's right back leg. Then fighter hooks the adversary's right leg by the abrupt movement of left leg back. Fighter's hands in grip with neck press down, so the adversary's structure is undercut.

The adversaries are in right-side stands. The adversary strikes blow by the right hand. Fighter deviates to the right and blocks the adversary's hand by the left forearm from inside. At once after block the same hand catches neck and the right one catches the adversary's left hand as it is shown on the figure. Right leg is taken forward behind the adversary's front leg. Then fighter hooks the adversary's left leg by the abrupt movement of right leg back. Fighter's hands in grip press down, so the adversary's structure is undercut.

The adversaries are in right-side stands. The adversary strikes blow by the right hand. Fighter deviates to the right-back and blocks the adversary's hand by the left forearm from inside. At once after block the hand catches elbow or forearm of adversary's striking hand. Synchronously the right hand makes grip of adversary's neck from the right side (relative to fighter). Right leg is taken forward behind the adversary's front leg. Then fighter hooks the adversary's left leg by the abrupt movement of right leg back. Fighter's hands in grip press down, so the adversary's structure is undercut.

THE INTERNAL HOOK
Basic variant

The practicing persons are in front of each other in side stands and elbow grips. Fighter transfers the weight on the front left leg, synchronously he forces adversary to transfer the body weight on his back right leg by this movement through the management of adversary's structure in elbow grip. Synchronously the fighter's right leg is taken from inside behind the adversary's left front leg. The adversary's structure is undercut with fall at the expanse of hooking swing by the right leg back and push by hands in elbow grip forward.

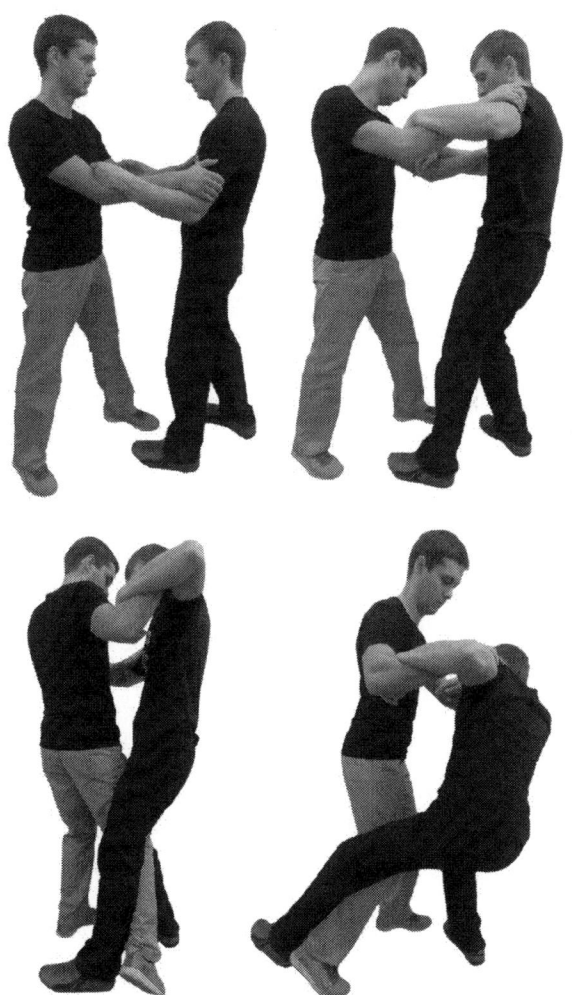

The adversaries are in right-side stands. The fighter makes step forward by the left leg. His right hand passes along the adversary's central line and builds the bridge from internal side of adversary's left hand, making grip of elbow or shoulder. Left hand covers the adversary's right one and makes grip. Then the fighter takes the right leg forward between the adversary's legs and hooks the adversary's front left one from internal side. Then he hooks the adversary's left leg by the abrupt movement of right leg back. Fighter's hands in grip press down, so the adversary's structure is undercut.

The adversaries are in right-side stands. The fighter makes step forward by the left leg and makes clinch of adversary's neck by the right hand. Left hand covers the adversary's right one and makes grip. Synchronously with grip the fighter takes the right leg forward between the adversary's legs and hooks the adversary's front left one from internal side. Then he hooks the adversary's left leg by the abrupt movement of right leg back. Fighter's hands in grip press down, so the adversary's structure is undercut.

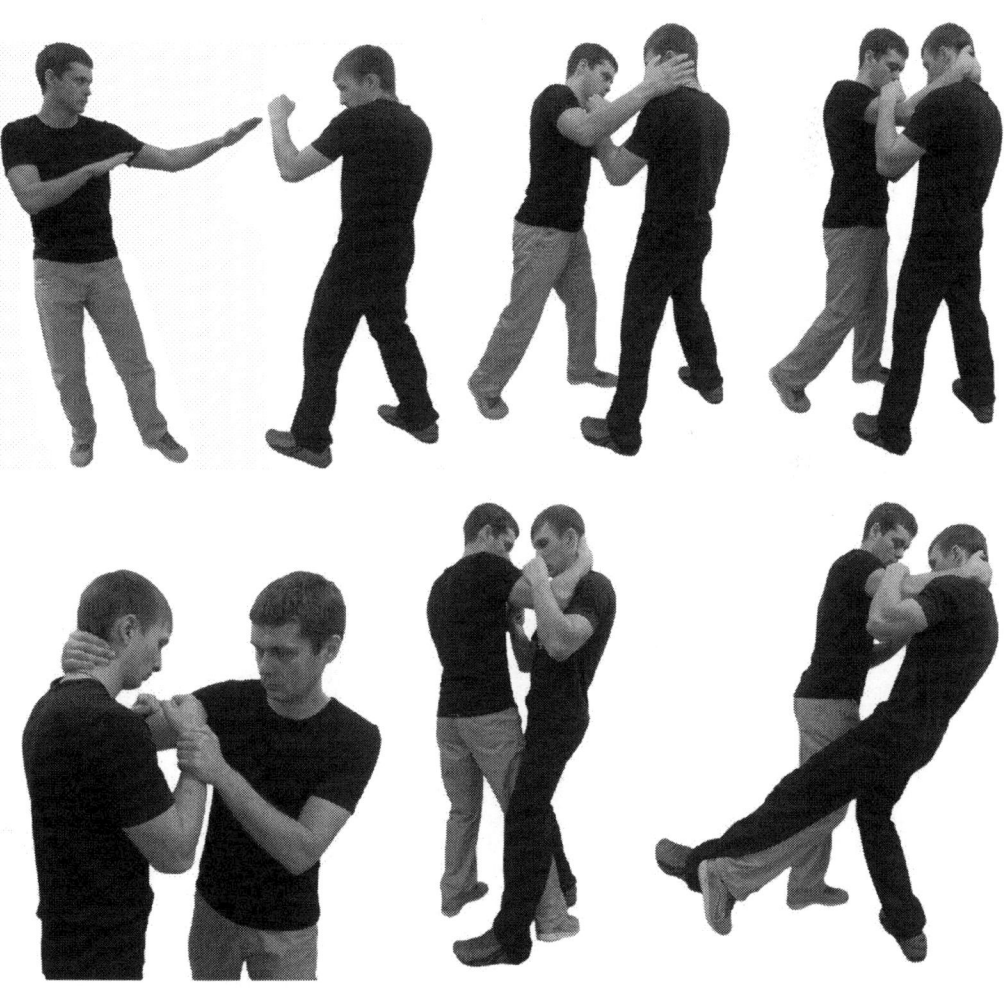

The adversaries are in right-side stands. Adversary strikes blow by the left hand. The fighter makes step forward and to the left by the left leg and blocks the adversary's hand by the right forearm from inside. At once after block through the technique of sticky hands fighter makes grip of adversary's hand. At that the left hand is laid on adversary's right one and catches it. Synchronously with grip the right leg is taken forward between the adversary's legs and hooks the adversary's front left one from inside. Then the fighter hooks the adversary's left leg by the abrupt movement of right leg back. Fighter's hands in grip press forward-down, so the adversary's structure is undercut.

The adversaries are in right-side stands. Adversary strikes blow by the left hand. The fighter makes step forward by the left leg and blocks the adversary's hand by the left forearm from external side. At once after block through the technique of sticky hands the fighter makes jerk of adversary's structure on himself as it is shown on the figure. At that the right hand is laid on the shoulder of adversary's striking hand for more firm control. Synchronously with grip the right leg is taken forward between the adversary's legs and hooks the adversary's front left one from inside. Then the fighter hooks the adversary's left leg by the abrupt movement of right leg back. Fighter's hands in grip press forward-down, so the adversary's structure is undercut.

The adversaries are in right-side stands. Adversary strikes blow by the right hand. The fighter makes step forward by the left leg, deviates to the left and blocks the adversary's hand by the right forearm from external side of striking hand. At once after block through the technique of sticky hands the fighter makes grip of adversary's hand as it is shown on the figure. At that the left hand is laid on the shoulder of adversary's striking hand for more firm control. Synchronously with grip the right leg is taken forward between the adversary's legs and hooks the adversary's front left one from inside. Then the fighter hooks the adversary's left leg by the abrupt movement of right leg back. Fighter's hands in grip press forward-down, so the adversary's structure is undercut.

Made in United States
Orlando, FL
31 January 2022